David Tuck
A Story of Holocaust Survival

As reported by Lise Marlowe

This book is dedicated to my family

Lise Marlowe is a 6th grade teacher at Elkins Park School in Cheltenham School District. She was named the national History Channel "Teacher of the Year" in 2006. Mrs. Marlowe received the award from First Lady Laura Bush at the White House along with a grant to continue saving local history with her students. The History Channel sent Mrs. Marlowe to join Mrs. Bush at the 2006 Preserve America Youth Summit in New Orleans where Mrs. Marlowe co-wrote a plan to preserve local history for educators.

Other awards Mrs. Marlowe received include the Pennsylvania Council for the Social Studies Elementary Teacher of the Year Award and the NAACP Freedom Fund Award. Mrs. Marlowe is currently serving as Chair of the Education Committee at the Holocaust Awareness Museum in Philadelphia. Other books Mrs. Marlowe has written include, "Back in Time with Cheltenham," "Frederick Douglass' Dream: The Story of the United States Colored Troops," "Renate: A Jewish girl who escaped Nazi Germany," and "Bringing beauty into the world: The life of Harry Somers."

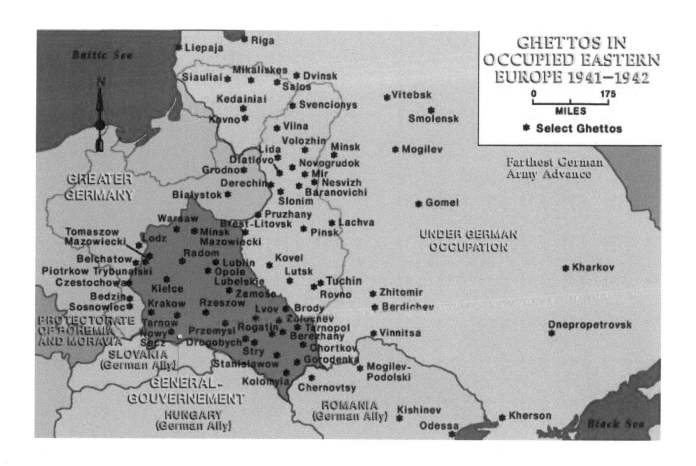

The Germans established at least 1,000 ghettos in German-occupied
and annexed Poland and the Soviet Union alone.

David's parents, Morris and Paula Tuch (original name)

David (infant) with grandparents and Uncle Abraham

Zdunska Wola, Poland

David Tuck was a young Jewish boy living a happy life in Poland unaware of the terror that was on the border of his beloved country. David was born in Zdunska Wola, Poland. There were over three million Jews living in Poland in 1939. Poland was home to the largest and most significant Jewish community in the world. Since Poland was where the majority of Europe's Jews lived at the time, this was where the German Nazi program for the extermination of Jews, the "Final Solution," was implemented. The plan was introduced by Heinrich Himmler and administered by Adolf Eichmann, the policy resulted in the murder of six million Jews.

David lost his mother, Pola, when he was only sixth months old. His orthodox grandparents, Sybil and Jehuda, took him in and gave him a public and hebrew education. When David was eight years old, he moved in with his father, Morris, stepmother, Luba, and half siblings, Karola, Fela and Ben for two years. His family was one of twelve Jewish families living in Jarocin, Poland, a small town bordering Germany. One evening the family heard their radio change from Polish music to German propaganda, *Deutschland Über Alles*, "Germany for the Whole World." On September 1, 1939, Adolf Hitler and the German Nazis invaded Poland and planned to destroy all Jewish communities. The Nazis burned down all Polish synagogues and arrested innocent Jewish men. David was only ten years old when his happy young life would suddenly become a nightmare.

Dworzec kolejowy.

Railway used to transport David and his family to Lodz Ghetto

Lodz Ghetto

The Nuremberg Race Laws were laws brutally enforced by the Nazis which excluded Jews from being citizens and took away their natural rights. Germans ordered registration of all European Jews and a word "*Jude*" was stamped in their identity cards. One of the laws that David was forced to follow was wearing the yellow star of David on his front and back to identify himself as a Jew. Another law said that Jews were forbidden to walk on the sidewalk, so he had to walk in the street if he saw a German officer. David would say to himself, "Why me? Why??" David was unaware at such a young age the hatred Nazis had towards the Jewish people. He didn't know that the Nazis had a "final solution" plan to terrorize and kill every Jewish person in Europe.

David was forced to work unloading cement bags from a train. One day as he was working, he saw Heinrich Himmler, the Nazi leader of the dreaded S.S., men who perceived themselves as the "racial elite" of Nazi future. A few weeks after the Nazis invaded Poland, David and his family were told they had to leave their home. They only had 48 hours to prepare for the relocation. The family was deported to Lodz Ghetto. Lodz Ghetto was a ghetto established by Nazi German authorities for Polish Jews. It was the second largest ghetto in German occupied Europe. The ghetto was transformed into an industrial center for manufacturing war supplies for Nazi Germany. Over 240,000 Jews passed through Lodz, but only 877 remained when the war was over. Prisoners were sent to Auschwitz and Chelmno extermination camps where most were murdered upon arrival.

Lodz Ghetto

When David arrived in Lodz, his family lived with another woman and David had to sleep on a table. Since David spoke German well enough, he was able to work in the food rations office providing families with food rations. It also helped that David spoke German because it allowed him to take every opportunity when talking to his captors to praise the Fatherland and Hitler. Many Jewish people knew German because they spoke Yiddish, a German dialect.

Life in Lodz Ghetto was unbearable for young David who spent two years as a prisoner. The Jews were entirely dependent on the German authorities for food, medicine and other vital supplies. Germans tried to starve the Jewish victims with small amounts of bread, potatoes and fat. It was common for people to trade valuables for food or beg to survive. David remembers always being hungry. Overcrowding was also common. One apartment may have several families living in it. Plumbing broke down and human waste lined the streets with the garbage. Contagious diseases spread quickly because of the cramped, unsanitary housing. Escape was impossible since there was heavy security.

During the long winters, heat was scarce and people wore rags to try to escape the cold. People would freeze to death in their sleep and bodies would line the streets for days waiting for removal. Tens of thousands died in the ghettos from illness and starvation. Death was everywhere and it became normal to see dead bodies in the ghetto. Every day children became orphaned, and many had to take care of even younger children. Orphans often lived on the streets, begging for bits of bread from others who had little or nothing to share.

Lodz Ghetto deported victims in cattle cars

Germans arrive in Posen, Poland

In the Spring of 1941, David was deported to Posen labor camp in Western Poland. When the Nazis came to Posen, they confiscated Jewish owned stores and businesses. They killed Jewish and Polish patients in the mental hospital. Jewish prisoners were used as forced labourers in public works, construction, gardening and transport projects throughout the city. Most of them had to sleep outdoors in appalling conditions. There was terror, starvation and disease.

David was assigned prisoner number, 176, at the Stadium on Dolna Wilda Street. He became a number, not a human being. Over 1,000 people were in Posen labor camp. Life at the stadium was unbearable, David lived in the building for two years. When he arrived, he lied about his age so he could work, claiming to be fifteen when he was only twelve. Children deemed too young to work were killed. David was chosen as one of ten boys to collect trash and were threatened with death if they brought any food back to the camp. He and the other boys would find scraps of food to eat. Even though they knew the risk, food was non existent and was calculated to starve the Jews. One day, three of the ten boys from David's group were missing. People at the camp and David were herded into a stadium, where they watched as the three young boys were hung.

Young David's daily life in the camp consisted of being woken up at 4am to take a shower and given a slice of bread and coffee. After his long work day, he was given another slice of bread at night and soup which was mostly made of water. This was his life for over 5 ½ years. He was forced by Gestapo at gunpoint to work at the cemetery to take out jewelry, crosses and gold teeth from the deceased and give to the officers. This awful experience led David to question his faith during his years of imprisonment. There were times when he said, "God, please choose someone else for a change."

Gates of Auschwitz

Women and child selected for gas chamber

In 1943, the Nazis liquidated the Posen labor camp and sent David for hard labor to construct an autobahn, which was like the turnpike. It is estimated that at least 10,000 people were sent to the 24 work camps established along the *autobahn*. Living conditions created by the German administration in the camp included terror, hunger, exhausting work, flogging, and public executions. Food was of poor quality and so was the clothing, which contributed to the high death rate. David chopped stones and dirt which was hard work. He used his wit and personality to stay alive and thought to ask the foreman if he needed help, suggesting he could clean his place, make his bed in the morning and clean his boots. The foreman agreed and David didn't have to chop anymore. The foreman would also leave bread and food from the kitchen which helped in David's hunger.

On August 25, 1943, David was sent to a sub camp in Auschwitz called Eintrachthütte, with other skilled workers. Auschwitz, also known as Auschwitz-Birkenau, opened in 1940 and was the largest of the Nazi concentration and death camps. More people died in Auschwitz than the British and American losses in World War II combined. As he entered the camp, he saw a sign at the entrance that said "Arbeit Macht Frei," which meant "work will set you free." This was a lie that the Nazis tricked the victims to believe. David would say to others, "if you work, you go to the chimney, the only way to go free was to die there," When he arrived in Auschwitz, he heard Bach music being played. He also saw women and children in one line and men in the other being selected for work or for death.

Children in Auschwitz

In Auschwitz, David was given a cup, plate and striped uniform. He recalled being skin and bones and using the plate as his pillow. He worked in a factory building anti-aircraft guns. On his arm, he was tattooed with the number 141631. He was then given a shaved haircut with a stripe cut in the middle. He sometimes worked with a fever and hid his illness so he wouldn't be selected for the gas chamber. He always worked even when he felt ill, knowing that the Nazi guards executed anyone too sick to work. He walked around like a zombie at times. When David went to sleep, he prayed to God, "Please let me see the light in the morning." Sometimes David would wake up and find the guy next to him dead.

The camp had wooden barracks for prisoners and was surrounded with double fenced high voltage barbed wire. There were Jews from all the European countries. Since there was no communication with the outside world, they didn't know what was going on and if they would ever be free. David used his wit again to survive and asked the commander if he could help in the control room. At the time, David's work was filing metal and he thought he could do more. David's smart thinking helped his situation because the commander agreed and left him bread.

One time, David hid a piece of bread in his shirt before he went to sleep at night and in the morning it was gone. People often stole from each other when starvation was unbearable. One day, for some reason, David put a piece of bread in a drawer in the factory where he worked and not in his shirt. Ten minutes later, a guard hit David from the back and he ended up on the floor. He got up and the guard asked what was in the drawer. He told the guard that it was bread. He asked where he got it and he said, "I got it from a Czechoslovakian."

```
T U C H      David                    58 800

                  1920                      -
       6.12.1922  Zdunska Wola Pol.          poln .
                  1924
1.     6.11.39-14.4.40  Sammellg. Lodz
       15.4.40-30.4.41  Gh. Lodz
        1.5.41-   8.43  Arbeitslg. Posen
        8.43-14.1.45    Auschwitz
       15.1.45-   3.45  Buchenwald
        3.45-15.4.45    Bergen-Belsen
2. befreit in Mauthausen-Gusen

Reg.Pr. Hann.
   23.6.67                           17.7.67
                                        ro
```

Documentation showing David's deportations

David would often hide bread in his shirt and take it out occasionally to nibble on it. He was afraid if he ate the bread too fast, that he would be hungry. To get more food, David and a Czechoslovakian man struck a deal while at Auschwitz. David would give the man his two weekly cigarettes if he gave him some of his food. Sometimes he was so hungry, he would boil grass and eat it.

One day, David was taken to see the commander, but he asked commander if he could get back to work so he could help make guns for "our Fatherland." The commander looked up at David and started laughing at him. David thought he was going to get the bullet, but the commander said, "Go back to work. Work for our Fatherland, but the next time you come here I will hang you upside down.'" David recalled this dramatic moment. "I said to myself, 'I'm alive.' From that moment on, I knew I was predestined and that I would survive."

On January 17, 1945, Auschwitz closed and David was once again deported to a concentration camp, Mauthausen in Austria. It was a brutal 370 mile train ride that took over five days. David and hundreds of other victims on the cattle car had no food, water, or bathroom during the terrifying journey. To survive, David tore his shirt into strips and tied a red tin cup that he had from camp to his belt, he dangled it out a narrow window and scooped snow from the ground. People were dying in the cattle car around him and the stench was terrible. He drank the melted snow and didn't share, there are no friends when you are trying to survive.

The U.S. 11th Armored Division liberating
Mauthausen-Gusen concentration camp

When David arrived in Mauthausen, he was stripped naked in twenty degrees weather. He thought he was going to die because it was so cold. The Nazis had the Jews shower and sleep on the bare floor. The inmates at Mauthausen–Gusen were forced to work as slave labor, under conditions that caused many deaths. The subcamps of the Mauthausen complex included quarries, munitions factories, mines, arms factories and plants assembling fighter aircraft. To accommodate the ever-growing number of slave workers, additional subcamps of Mauthausen were built. By the end of the war, the list included 101 camps.

The sub camp David was sent to was Güsen II. He worked in an underground factory to build German aircraft. With no food, he boiled grass in water to eat. One day, there was a roll call where they had the inmates line up and stand for long periods of time. They were told that they were going to be free, but they needed to stay in the barracks or they would be killed. David could hear guns shooting outside the barracks as the Americans tanks approached the camp. David doesn't know how he survived such harsh conditions and unbearable treatment by the Nazis.

On May 5, 1945, the U.S. 11th Armored Division arrived at the Mauthausen-Gusen concentration camp and David was finally liberated. David was only 78 pounds at 15 years old and looked like a skeleton. He had no strength and could barely walk. But he was free and alive. He survived on bread, weak coffee, watered down soup for more than five years. The Americans warned the survivors to not overeat even though they were starving. Since David was so malnourished, overeating would kill him. Soon after the war, David had nightmares about his terrifying treatment by the Nazis. He no longer dreams of the horrors, but he does still vividly recall what he went through.

David's Displaced Persons camp document

David and Marie leaving Europe for America

David spent many months in a Displaced Persons camp recuperating from his malnutrition in the concentration camps. Displaced Persons camps were established after World War II for refugees from Eastern Europe and for the former inmates of the Nazi German concentration camps. Some Holocaust survivors were contained in the camps for up to a year because of the diseases they contracted during their imprisonment. Some people died in refugee camps because they overate or were heartbroken from losing their family. David's injuries were a bump on his head from a beating. To this day, David still has the numbers 141631 on his arm. David was one of the few survivors from Poland. Over ninety percent of the Polish Jews would be murdered in Nazi extermination camps or died by starvation in the ghettos.

David found out several years after the war that his dad, stepmother and half-sister, Fela, survived the camps. Communication for survivors was very difficult and it took years for family members to find each other. David eventually came to America in 1950 with his wife, Marie Roza, who he met in Paris and was also a Holocaust survivor. She was in a concentration camp making clothing for the German army. Marie was a beautiful singer and David called her "my tchotchke", which means something special. David and Marie moved to Brooklyn with nothing and then to Philadelphia. They were married for 54 years and had a daughter.

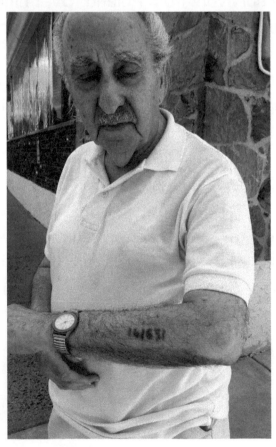

For many years, David has brought his story of survival and perseverance to thousands of students around the nation. For many years David didn't talk about the Holocaust, but now feels educating the youth is important to make sure the history of what happened to the Jewish people is not forgotten. There are many people who deny the Holocaust happened. David lived through it for over 5 ½ years and is proof that deniers are liars. David will never forget or forgive the Nazis for what they did to him and his family, but he won't give them the satisfaction of hating them. "Hate only destroys your life." David lived a good life after the war because he was happy to be alive. His Jewish faith has only grown stronger since he survived. There were times that he said, "God, thank you."

When David speaks to students about his experience, he tells them, "Live life the best you can. When you wake up in the morning and see the light, be happy. If you have life, you have hope." David also talks about bullying which affects American schools. He says that Hitler was the biggest bully. "If somebody gives you trouble. Don't say anything. Walk away. I prayed every day for five and a half years just to live until the next day. How can one bully twist the mind?" Our students are the last generation to meet a Holocaust survivor, they must never forget the horrors of the Nazi regime and stand up if anyone claims the Holocaust didn't happen. Listening to David Tuck's story is vital for our youth to hear so that they will teach their children and future generations about the horrors of the Holocaust.

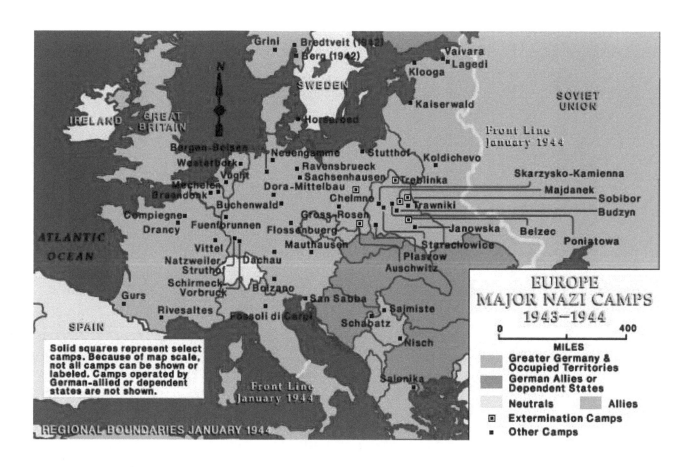

Between 1933 and 1945, Nazi Germany and its allies established more than 40,000 camps and other incarceration sites.

REFUGEE/DISPLACED PERSON STATISTICAL CARD

29.9.50. to *Grohn*

Form C/M/I/A

482851

1. Surname

Tüch

2. Christian Names

David

3. Sex (Male/Female)

male

4. D.P. Identity Card No.

5. Family Status, Family Head Family member Unaccompanied under 17 Unattached 17 and over (If Family member give name of Family Head)

6. If Family Head, state number in Family

4

7. IRO Eligibility

Status mandate of I.R.O.

protection including repatriation and resettlement

1.12.49

8. Reason for evic-
Date on of leaving I.O. Area Office
Camp

Emigrated to: USA on 29. 9. 50. u/a Grohn

9. Date of Origin of Card

1.12.49

10. Country of Citizenship or Ethnic Origin

Poland

11. Country of Last Habitual Residence

Poland

12. Religion

Jew

13. Place and Date of Birth

Tdünska / Pol.

14. Present Location. D.P. Camp/ CMLO / CMWS / German Economy (If in D.P. Camp state Assembly No.)

D.P. Camp Belsen

15. If in Hospital, Home, Foster Home or Centre other than a D.P. Camp state place name.

David's emigration card to United States in 1950

"If you have life, you have hope".......David Tuck

The Holocaust Awareness Museum
Celebrates the Contributions

of

Dave Tuck

In honor of doing over 500 survivor programs,
reaching over 50,000 students and raising
thousands of dollars for our important mission

You have our eternal admiration and love!

Chuck Feldman, President   June, 2016

To learn more about David Tuck's story
visit The Holocaust Awareness Museum
Philadelphia, Pennsylvania
www.hamec.org

ISBN:
978-1-387-15751-8